M000074654

AN IDEAS INTO ACTION GUIDEBOOK

Feedback That Works for Nonprofit Organizations

Copyright © 2013 Center for Creative Leadership. All Rights Reserved.

IDEAS INTO ACTION GUIDEBOOKS

Aimed at managers and executives who are concerned with their own and others' development, each guidebook in this series gives specific advice on how to complete a developmental task or solve a leadership problem.

LEAD CONTRIBUTOR	Shera Clark
CONTRIBUTORS	Anand Chandrasekar
	Karen Dyer
	Lynn Fick-Cooper
	John Fleenor
	Kelly Hannum
	Nancy Henjum
	Emily Hoole
	Sandrine Tunezerwe
	Hughes Van Stichel
DIRECTOR OF ASSESSMENTS, TOOLS, AND PUBLICATIONS	Sylvester Taylor
MANAGER, PUBLICATION DEVELOPMENT	Peter Scisco
EDITORS	Stephen Rush, Karen Lewis
ASSOCIATE EDITOR	Shaun Martin
ASSISTANT EDITOR	Joan Bello
DESIGN AND LAYOUT	Joanne Ferguson
COVER DESIGN	Laura J. Gibson
	Chris Wilson, 29 & Company
RIGHTS AND PERMISSIONS	Kelly Lombardino

Copyright © 2013 Center for Creative Leadership.

All Rights Reserved. No part of this publication may be reproduced, stored in a retrieval system, or transmitted, in any form or by any means, electronic, mechanical, photocopying, recording, or otherwise, without the prior written permission of the publisher. Printed in the United States of America.

CCL No. 460
ISBN No. 978-1-60491-172-5

CENTER FOR CREATIVE LEADERSHIP
WWW.CCL.ORG

Copyright © 2013 Center for Creative Leadership. All Rights Reserved.

AN IDEAS INTO ACTION GUIDEBOOK

Feedback That Works for Nonprofit Organizations

Shera Clark

Center for
Creative
Leadership®

Copyright © 2013 Center for Creative Leadership. All Rights Reserved.

THE IDEAS INTO ACTION GUIDEBOOK SERIES

This series of guidebooks draws on the practical knowledge that the Center for Creative Leadership (CCL) has generated since its inception in 1970. The purpose of the series is to provide leaders with specific advice on how to complete a developmental task or solve a leadership challenge. In doing that, the series carries out CCL's mission to advance the understanding, practice, and development of leadership for the benefit of society worldwide.

CCL's unique position as a research and education organization supports a community of accomplished scholars and educators in a community of shared knowledge. CCL's knowledge community holds certain principles in common, and its members work together to understand and generate practical responses to the ever-changing circumstances of leadership and organizational challenges.

In its interactions with a richly varied client population, in its research into the effect of leadership on organizational performance and sustainability, and in its deep insight into the workings of organizations, CCL creates new, sound ideas that leaders all over the world put into action every day. We believe you will find the Ideas Into Action Guidebooks an important addition to your leadership toolkit.

Copyright © 2013 Center for Creative Leadership. All Rights Reserved.

Table of Contents

Copyright © 2013 Center for Creative Leadership. All Rights Reserved.

IN BRIEF

In nonprofit organizations, staff development is increasingly crucial, but lack of resources leads many nonprofit leaders to believe that effective feedback systems are unattainable. However, nonprofits can implement effective feedback through their organizations by taking advantage of the Situation-Behavior-Impact (SBI) model.

The first step of SBI is to capture the specific situation in which the behavior occurred. This specificity creates context for your feedback recipient, so he or she can clearly associate the behavior with a place and time. Second, describe the behavior, but not the person. For example, rather than saying that a person was rude, describe what the person did that was rude (interrupted you, did not pay attention to your questions, and so forth). This prevents people from perceiving that you are judging them, and instead gives them specific actions that they need to reflect on. Finally, discuss the impact that the person's behavior had on you, and what your reaction to that behavior was. This sharing of perspective increases trust and communication between you and the recipient, and strengthens the probability that your feedback will be understood.

Using this system, you can give effective feedback that will help your nonprofit achieve its mission.

Copyright © 2013 Center for Creative Leadership. All Rights Reserved.

Effective Feedback and Nonprofit Organizations

Effective feedback is an important and efficient way to let people know the impact of their behavior so they are able to make informed choices regarding future actions. Feedback is also a way to help people who work together do so more efficiently, because it creates open communication, which allows for frank discussions regarding problems and concerns.

Effective feedback consists of crafting a simple and direct message about behavior that separates what happened from how we think or feel about it, reduces uncertainty and ambiguity, and provides actionable information rather than messages that have to be interpreted. Such feedback can also help individuals make better choices about their behavior and help people work together more efficiently, because it fosters open and direct communication. It also provides people with tangible information about how their actions have had an impact on others. People are likely to change ineffective behaviors if they realize they are having a negative impact or understand exactly what it is they are doing that is getting in the way. Effective feedback empowers people with the information they need in order to know whether they are having the impact they want.

Nonprofit organizations increasingly see staff development as a critical goal in their work. In most if not all nonprofit organizations, staff members are the reason the mission is achieved (or not). Even if your development budget is nonexistent, effective

Effective feedback empowers people with the information they need in order to know whether they are having the impact they want.

Copyright © 2013 Center for Creative Leadership. All Rights Reserved.

feedback can be a low-cost and simple way to develop yourself and the people you work with. Effective feedback can also be part of a larger development effort in service of your organization's mission.

The work of nonprofit organizations is challenging, particularly as the contexts within which they work are increasingly complex and the people with whom they work may have different backgrounds and perspectives. In such a diverse environment, utilizing effective feedback is essential in facilitating successful communication across backgrounds and boundaries. This guidebook will show you how to use such feedback in your organization, and how to establish feedback systems that will continue to contribute to your nonprofit's overall mission and effectiveness as an organization.

What Is Effective Feedback?

The key to effective feedback is the ability to create and deliver a specific message based on observed behavior. This kind of message enables the receiver to walk away understanding exactly what he or she did and what impact it had on you. When feedback is specific and direct, there is a good chance that the person getting the feedback will be motivated to begin, continue, or stop behaviors that impact effectiveness. Think about statements you have made to others concerning their behavior, and ask yourself: What did they do that made you think they were good leaders? What did they say and how did they say it to make you think they communicate well? What did they do that made you conclude their thinking wasn't strategic enough?

In the pages that follow you will learn how to answer such questions as you develop your feedback skills. After you have read this guidebook, you will be able to

Copyright © 2013 Center for Creative Leadership. All Rights Reserved.

- give feedback that accurately represents your thoughts without blame or judgment
- become more conscious of a person's behavior and the messages it sends
- increase your awareness of the emotional responses you have to the actions of others
- be able to ask for more effective feedback that you can use for your own development

Common Pitfalls

During many CCL programs, we ask leaders, "How many of you give good, consistent feedback to the people you work with?" Usually, only one or two people raise their hands. Why so few? The reasons are varied: "It's hard to do," "I am afraid I will say something I will regret," "People get emotional when they hear things they don't like," "It might jeopardize my work relationships." All of these concerns are valid, but they all stem from common mistakes that people make when giving feedback.

The feedback judges individuals, not actions. The number one mistake people make in giving feedback is putting it in judgmental terms. If you say to someone, "You were too abrasive" or "You need to be a better team player," you send a strong message about what you think is right or wrong and that you've judged this person as falling short of expectations. Judgmental feedback puts people on the defensive. By the time the words are out of your mouth, your feedback recipient is already thinking, "Who do you think you are, calling me abrasive?" The energy spent in defense from your attack defeats any chance of a useful conversation.

The feedback is too vague. The second most common mistake made in giving feedback is the use of generalized, cliché

Copyright © 2013 Center for Creative Leadership. All Rights Reserved.

catchphrases: "You are a good leader," "You did a great job on the presentation," "You are one of our best volunteers." People hearing these words may be happy to get the compliment, but they will not know exactly what they did to earn your praise. If you want to encourage people to repeat efficient behavior, you have to let them know what they did well so they can keep doing it.

The feedback speaks for others. Saying something like "Sheila said that you seem confused about your new assignment" or "People are telling me that they feel that you are micromanaging them" isn't providing effective feedback. At best, recipients will be perplexed by such statements and wonder who is talking about them. At worst, they may resent colleagues for going to someone else rather than giving the feedback directly. They are likely to become defensive and unable to accept your feedback.

The feedback gives unwanted advice. If you give advice with your feedback, the receiver may think you have a personal agenda. When you say something like "Let me tell you what you need to do to have a successful team meeting," you immediately put listeners on the defensive, because they may interpret your statement as "You don't know how to have a team meeting, so let me explain it to you." This kind of statement can come across as belittling and insulting.

Negative feedback gets sandwiched between positive messages. If you have to give negative feedback, it is tempting to start the conversation with something positive, then deliver a negative statement, and then soothe the situation with another positive message (a good-bad-good sandwich). Consider the following: "I was really impressed with your presentation today, though I think several of your points were misleading and incorrect. Regardless, I think you really impressed the senior staff." Your

Copyright © 2013 Center for Creative Leadership. All Rights Reserved.

intentions may be good, but you are mistaken if you think people hearing this kind of feedback get a clear message. Instead, the recipient will soon figure out what you are doing, filter out the two positive ends, and focus on the negative message in the middle— or get confused and not take the negative statement seriously.

The feedback is exaggerated. Another key mistake is using words like *always* and *never*. Hearing these words, people naturally get defensive, as they can remember plenty of times when they did not do what you claim they did.

The behavior is labeled as a problem. If you label the behavior as a problem, you put the receiver on the defensive and your message may not be understood. When you say, "You have a problem getting your board reports in on time," the person listening will immediately get defensive and, instead of attempting to understand your feedback, may try to explain or justify the problem. Your message will be interpreted as an attack, rather than a contribution to his or her professional development.

Delivering Effective Feedback

CCL has developed a feedback technique called Situation-Behavior-Impact, or SBI. Using this technique, which CCL teaches to thousands of leaders every year, you can deliver feedback that replaces personal attacks, incorrect judgments, vague statements, and third-party slights with direct and objective comments on a person's actions. Hearing this kind of feedback, the recipient can see what actions he or she can take to continue to improve performance or to change behavior that is ineffective or even an obstacle to performance.

Copyright © 2013 Center for Creative Leadership. All Rights Reserved.

S Situation
Grounded in time and place

B Behavior
Physical, observable action

I Impact
What I felt/thought/did

©2012 Center for Creative Leadership. All Rights Reserved.

The SBI technique works because it is simple and direct. When giving feedback, you capture the situation, describe the behavior you observed, and then explain the impact that the behavior had on you. In the following pages, we will show you how to use each component of the SBI approach.

Capture the Situation

The first step in giving effective feedback is to capture and clarify the specific situation in which the behavior occurred. If you say, "On Tuesday, in the break room with Carol and Fred" rather than "A couple days ago at the office with everybody," you avoid the kind of vague comments and exaggerations that derail many feedback opportunities. Describing the location and time of a behavior creates context for your feedback recipients, helping them clearly remember their thinking and behavior at the time.

Remember that capturing the situation is only the start of your feedback session. Here are a few examples of how you might successfully describe a situation when giving feedback:

- "Yesterday, when you presented our fund-raising strategy to the board . . ."

- "Last Monday, after lunch, while we were walking with Cindy to the meeting . . ."

- "Today, first thing this morning, when you and I were talking at the coffee machine . . ."

12

Copyright © 2013 Center for Creative Leadership. All Rights Reserved.

- "This past Tuesday afternoon, at the welcome reception for the new program manager, when Karl was explaining his new job description . . ."

Specificity is important when recalling a situation. The more specifics and details you can use in bringing the situation to mind, the clearer your message will be.

Describe the Behavior

Describing behavior is the second step in giving effective feedback. It's also the most crucial step—and the one most often omitted—because behavior can be difficult to identify and describe. The most common mistake in giving feedback happens when judgments are communicated using adjectives that describe a person but not a person's actions. This is ineffective because it does not give the receiver information about what behavior to begin, continue, or stop in order to improve performance. Consider the statements below:

- "He was rude during the meeting."
- "She was engaged during the small-group discussion."
- "She seemed bored at her team's presentation."
- "He seemed pleased with the report his employees presented."

These statements describe an observer's impression or interpretation of a behavior. Now look at the following list of actions an observer might witness that would lead to those impressions and interpretations.

- "He spoke at the same time another person was speaking." (rude)
- "She leaned forward in her chair, wrote notes after other people spoke, and then shared her thoughts with the

13

Copyright © 2013 Center for Creative Leadership. All Rights Reserved.

group, referring to some of the things that other people had said." (engaged)

- "She yawned, rolled her eyes, and looked out the window." (bored)

- "He smiled and nodded his head." (pleased)

The statements in this list use verbs to describe a person's actions. The focus is on the actual behavior, not on a judgment as to what the behavior might mean. If you remember to use verbs when describing behavior, you avoid the mistake of judging behavior. By focusing on the action, not the impression, you can communicate clear, specific facts that a person can understand and act on.

Use Worksheet 1, Behavior or Not Behavior—That Is the Question, to practice recognizing concrete description of behavior.

To become more adept at identifying behavior and, in turn, be better able to communicate what you have seen to the feedback recipient, you have to capture not only what people do but how they do it. The new executive director who stands before her organization and says "I am excited to be your new director" will appear insincere if she has no expression on her face, speaks in a flat voice, and uses no hand gestures. When giving people feedback using SBI, it is important to capture not only what is said and done but *how* it is said and done. You can capture the how by paying attention to body language, tone of voice and speaking manner, and word choice.

Body language. This nonverbal communication includes facial expressions, eye movement, body posture, and hand gestures. For example:

Jim became increasingly irritated with Alice during their meeting. Alice frequently shook her foot, shifted in her seat numerous times, looked at her phone repeatedly, and nodded

Copyright © 2013 Center for Creative Leadership. All Rights Reserved.

Worksheet 1: Behavior or Not Behavior—That Is the Question

Use a check mark to classify each item as Behavior or Not Behavior, and then summarize your reasoning in the Why column. See the key at the bottom of the worksheet for the correct answers.

Item	Behavior	Not Behavior	Why
1. You were aggressive.			
2. You suggested we do a matrix to sort out the options.			
3. You invited people to express their opinions and asked follow-up questions.			
4. You are not skilled at collaboration.			

15

Copyright © 2013 Center for Creative Leadership. All Rights Reserved.

Worksheet 1: Behavior or Not Behavior—That Is the Question (continued)

Item	Behavior	Not Behavior	Why
5. You are a good team player who cares about staff and volunteers.			
6. You interrupted her several times.			
7. Your attitude was threatening.			
8. You started the meeting by criticizing the team for its performance.			
9. You spoke twice during the 40-minute meeting.			

Key: Items 2, 3, 6, 8, and 9 are behaviors. Items 1, 4, 5, and 7 are not.

Copyright © 2013 Center for Creative Leadership. All Rights Reserved.

her head at people as they passed by Jim's cubicle while he was talking.

Although Alice never spoke, she sent loud and clear messages through her body language. Jim can give Alice effective feedback by saying something like the following:

"Alice, during our meeting yesterday in my cubicle, I noticed that you looked at your phone several times during a 15-minute period. You responded to your e-mail and shifted from side to side in your seat. You also nodded your head at people as they passed by my cubicle while I was speaking."

Jim has communicated the situation and many clear instances of behavior to Alice. His approach will help Alice understand the negative impact of her behavior (the final step of giving effective feedback).

Tone of voice and speaking manner. Included here are the pitch of a person's voice, the speed and volume at which the person speaks, and the pauses used when speaking. Broadcasters, especially sportscasters and news anchors, are masters of this. Voice mannerisms can be hard to notice and describe for the purpose of giving effective feedback, but are useful behavioral cues. For example:

Jason was introducing a new program idea to a group of his peers. During his presentation he paused on at least six different occasions, halting in midsentence. After these pauses, his voice slowed down considerably. He spoke in a low monotone. When people asked him questions, he suddenly spoke very fast. He ended his talk saying "Thank you! Thank you very much!" in a tone that was louder than he had used throughout the whole speech.

Copyright © 2013 Center for Creative Leadership. All Rights Reserved.

Some of the impressions you have of Jason may include uncertainty, nervousness, hesitancy, and lack of presentation skills. But to say just that to him doesn't help him develop. Effective feedback would include a description of Jason's speaking manner. You would talk about how he presented the material—the pauses and the speed and volume of his speech:

> "Jason, during your presentation yesterday you stopped several times and spoke so low that it was difficult for me to hear you. Then, toward the end of your presentation, when people asked questions, you spoke faster and your voice got louder. I wondered if you were prepared for the presentation, and when you spoke faster at the end, I felt rushed."

Word choice. This is often the least important component of behavior. Nevertheless, capturing the specific language a person uses during a situation can help you give effective feedback.

> During a video conferencing team meeting, Bob lost his temper when he learned that Fred would miss a deadline for a proposal. Bob called Fred lazy in front of the entire group. When the meeting ended, the team members quickly logged off without speaking to one another.

If the content of a person's message has an impact on you and you want to give effective feedback, write down the speaker's words so you can remember exactly what was said:

> "Bob, during the team meeting this morning you called Fred lazy in front of the whole group. I was really uncomfortable that you singled out one person and used that kind of language. After hearing that, I felt that we were not a team at all."

Copyright © 2013 Center for Creative Leadership. All Rights Reserved.

Points of Delivery

When attempting to give someone feedback, consider the following points in order to communicate your feedback successfully:

- When you approach someone to offer feedback, use a question such as "May I share an observation with you?" This open approach, in which you ask permission, can ease anxiety and sets the scene for a conversation, not a confrontation.

- To create more openness around the notion of feedback, say something positive, ask if the person understands what behavior you're talking about, and then stop talking and wait for a response. This positive approach can ease the fear many people have when they hear the word *feedback*.

- When providing negative feedback to someone, acknowledge the uneasiness or discomfort you may feel when giving a person feedback. Say something like "As I am telling you this, I'm aware of how uncomfortable I am." A simple acknowledgment honors your experience and can minimize the perceived threat of the feedback experience from the receiver's perspective.

Explain the Impact

The final step in giving effective feedback is to relay the impact that the other person's behavior had on you. The impact you want to communicate is not how you think a person's behavior might affect other people or the organization, but rather your reaction to a behavior. There are two directions you can take when sharing this impact:

Copyright © 2013 Center for Creative Leadership. All Rights Reserved.

- You can evaluate or make a judgment about the person's behavior: "I thought you showed interest when you asked for the group's opinions." This tactic is more common but also less effective because the person getting the feedback can argue with your interpretation of the behavior.

- You can acknowledge the emotional effect the person's behavior had on you. "When you told me in the meeting that my concerns about proposal deadlines were 'overblown,' I felt hurt." This approach can be more effective than the first because it is your reaction to someone's behavior, a reaction that only you experience. The person hearing your feedback cannot easily dismiss your personal experience, and so is more likely to hear what you've said.

By communicating the personal impact a behavior has had on you, you are sharing a point of view and asking the other person to view that behavior from your perspective. This kind of sharing helps to build trust, which in turn can lead to even more effective feedback as you improve your communication skills. If you have difficulty finding the right word to describe the impact a behavior has had on you, take a look at our list of impact words for help.

To develop your effectiveness in carrying out the impact stage of giving feedback, practice putting your feedback in the form of "When you did (behavior), I felt (impact)" or "When you said (behavior), I was (impact)." Here are some examples of how you might use this form when giving feedback. (The examples illustrate the entire SBI form, with the impact statement underlined.)

Peer feedback. "Sophie, this morning in the hallway you asked for my opinion about decisions to launch our annual campaign. You

Copyright © 2013 Center for Creative Leadership. All Rights Reserved.

Impact Words

These words can help you express the impact a behavior has had on you.

uncomfortable	uncertain	miserable
low	isolated	impressed
calm	vulnerable	annoyed
encouraged	rewarded	electrified
relieved	frantic	encouraged
skeptical	vehement	persecuted
lonely	sympathetic	ecstatic
jealous	fearful	worried
abandoned	sure	exhausted
important	hurt	restless
ignored	tired	unsettled
uninformed	glad	shocked
threatened	helpful	honored
angry	startled	welcome
coerced	supported	sad
happy	spiteful	flustered
challenged	disengaged	outraged

21

Copyright © 2013 Center for Creative Leadership. All Rights Reserved.

Impact Words (continued)

good	persuaded	proud
petrified	motivated	gratified
helpless	peaceful	uneasy
infuriated	excited	frustrated
diminished	betrayed	empty
troubled	pleasant	deserted
relaxed	satisfied	confident
tense	ambivalent	confused
astounded	bored	pressured
nervous	scared	belittled
wonderful	rejected	burdened
disturbed	inspired	captivated
neglected	overwhelmed	mad
pleased	left out	intimidated
refreshed	frightened	

By communicating the personal impact a behavior has had on you, you are sharing a point of view and asking the other person to view that behavior from your perspective.

Copyright © 2013 Center for Creative Leadership. All Rights Reserved.

also often ask me to join the group at lunch. <u>When you do that, I feel included, part of the team.</u>"

Direct report feedback. "Matt, in the meeting with the new vice president yesterday, you kept your voice at an even tone, even when she questioned your budget. <u>I felt really at ease with your delivery.</u>"

Volunteer feedback. "Leslie, over the past week you have been putting in extra volunteer hours to meet this upcoming deadline. <u>I really appreciate the time and effort you're putting into the organization.</u>"

Boss feedback. "Karen, I completed my reports a week ago, and you have not commented on them. <u>I do not feel acknowledged for the work I do.</u>"

Board feedback. "Bob, during Tuesday's board meeting, you called for a vote on the budget item Terry suggested without seeking my input first. <u>I felt dismissed and wondered if the board really understood the implications of that new expense.</u>"

Use Worksheet 2, Situation–Behavior–Impact Observation, to practice using the SBI model.

Additional Tools

In addition to the SBI model, you can employ additional methods in order to increase the effectiveness of your feedback.

Give your feedback in a timely manner. When people receive immediate (or almost immediate) feedback on an issue or situation, they are more likely to benefit. The incident is fresh in their minds, and they are more likely to make connections between your observations and what they need to improve on. If you wait

Copyright © 2013 Center for Creative Leadership. All Rights Reserved.

Worksheet 2: Situation–Behavior–Impact Observation

Think about a situation that has occurred in the past and led you to give feedback to someone. Using the SBI model, revisit how you would give that feedback.

1. What was the situation? Be specific.

2. What was the behavior? What did you observe the person doing? Remember to focus on the specific action the person took, not on your interpretation of the action (that the person was aggressive or rude, for example).

3. What was the impact of that behavior on you? How did you feel, or what did you think?

4. Now, reflect on the whole process. Practice combining your observations into a single paragraph or statement.

Copyright © 2013 Center for Creative Leadership. All Rights Reserved.

too long to give feedback, the situation may be so far out of their minds that they, while acknowledging your suggestions, benefit little from your help.

Give your feedback and then stop talking. Give people time to digest and understand your feedback, and do not overwhelm them with additional instructions or suggestions. Feedback is not a one-way street; it's a two-way process that requires work from both the person giving feedback and the person receiving it. If you do not give people a chance to be a part of the process, they may view your feedback as an attack rather than a discussion about their professional development.

Focus on a single message. By keeping your feedback specific, you increase the chance that people will absorb what you're saying and act on it. If you give them several suggestions at once, they may not know which to act on first, or which is most important. A single specific message limits confusion and will lead to a single direct response in return.

Putting It All Together

Review the situation, behavior, and impact steps of providing effective feedback and practice the steps as often as you can. You do not have to wait for an actual feedback situation to arise in order to review your skills. For example, the next time you attend a professional conference and hear a compelling presentation, think about what you are experiencing that makes the presentation so valuable. Observe the speaker and take note of the situation, the speaker's behavior, and the impact that behavior is having on you. Is the speaker using hand gestures? What about tone of voice? What

Copyright © 2013 Center for Creative Leadership. All Rights Reserved.

kinds of facial expressions is the speaker using? Are the speaker's words appropriate for the audience and the subject?

After you have practiced at a distance like this, practice with a willing partner, preferably someone at work. You can address a simple situation with a simple impact, but use an instance that really takes place (an imaginary situation will not be as relevant). State the facts (situation and behavior) and then give your response (impact).

Take time to reflect on your feedback efforts. Ask yourself, "Why did I pay attention to this particular behavior? What does this say about me?" Perhaps you have observed behaviors you want to develop in yourself or behaviors you want to drop or guard against. Reflection also gives you time to understand the true nature of the impact the behavior had on you. Ask yourself, "How did I feel when she talked to me in that tone of voice?" or "What emotional response did I have when he shook my hand and said my reports showed good research and attention to detail?" Reflection will help you become more concise and focused in delivering your feedback message, and help you avoid traps that weaken your message.

As you become more familiar with the approach and more comfortable with the delivery, your feedback skills will become more and more effective. The people you work with will benefit from the effort you put toward helping them develop. You, in turn, will benefit from developing a useful skill that not only helps to raise the effectiveness of the people around you but also bolsters your leadership skills.

As you become more familiar with the approach and more comfortable with the delivery, your feedback skills will become more and more effective.

Copyright © 2013 Center for Creative Leadership. All Rights Reserved.

What to Do and What Not to Do
When Giving Feedback

Do

✓ Be specific when recalling the situation.

✓ Be specific when describing the behavior.

✓ Acknowledge the impact of the behavior on you.

✓ Give feedback in a timely manner.

✓ Give your feedback and then stop talking.

✓ Focus on a single message.

Do Not

✓ Use accusations or judge the person.

✓ Pass along vague feedback from others.

✓ Give advice unless asked.

✓ Sandwich your negative feedback between positive messages.

✓ Generalize or exaggerate your feedback with words like *always* and *never*.

✓ Label a behavior as a problem.

Copyright © 2013 Center for Creative Leadership. All Rights Reserved.

The Importance of Feedback for Nonprofit Organizations

You cannot overstate the importance of effective feedback for an organization. Feedback allows members of an organization to receive direct, pertinent information on how they are performing and helps build cohesiveness. This consistency and focus only strengthens the work of the organization, and institutions lacking regular feedback often are disjointed, lacking the drive and singular commitment necessary to succeed in a competitive economy.

For nonprofit organizations, effective feedback is essential both for achieving the organization's mission and for promoting professional development. Nonprofits may not view feedback as an integral part of their mission, and they may choose to forego it in favor of more immediate demands, such as obtaining funding or pursuing other internal and external goals. However, we believe that nonprofits can use feedback throughout their organizations, even without having the funding for specialized feedback systems. For instance, you can use feedback in everyday situations and interactions, such as performance reviews, conversations with your direct reports and volunteers, and staff meetings, allowing feedback to serve as in-the-moment training for members of your organization. Furthermore, instead of seeing feedback as a way to harm existing relationships, you can use feedback to improve communication in your workplace and, ultimately, empower your colleagues. For example, consider the 80-20 rule when providing feedback in your organization. That is, 80 percent of the time you should give regular, positive feedback to employees and volunteers. Then if you need to give constructive feedback, they are more open to that feedback, and they feel that you see their value and

Copyright © 2013 Center for Creative Leadership. All Rights Reserved.

their need for development fairly. You don't need a formal system to engage in constructive feedback; rather, employ the suggestions and guidelines above, and you can turn feedback from a negative discussion into a developmental opportunity. If you can incorporate this kind of feedback into your organization's mission, you will find that achieving your goals is one step closer than you realized.

Background

The Center for Creative Leadership has conducted extensive research into developmental feedback, focusing on how utilizing assessment in conjunction with systematic feedback approaches can improve the leadership capabilities of an organization.

In particular, CCL's Leadership Development Program (LDP) emphasizes the value of collaboration across boundaries to effectively manage leaders. One way this collaboration can occur is through evaluation systems that effectively communicate issues or concerns with those receiving feedback. Furthermore, LDP utilizes and teaches in-the-moment peer feedback as a means of communicating issues or concerns, and participants learn firsthand how to improve their feedback skills.

CCL has also conducted research into nonprofit organizations and, in particular, the role that relationships, both within and without, can play in strengthening the organization and advancing its goals. An important part of these relationships is feedback, and nonprofit organizations may not have implemented effective feedback systems because of financial or other constraints. Working effective feedback techniques into a nonprofit's overall operation can help advance its mission and increase its capabilities.

Copyright © 2013 Center for Creative Leadership. All Rights Reserved.

Suggested Resources

Buron, R. J., & McDonald-Mann, D. (1999). *Giving feedback to subordinates.* Greensboro, NC: Center for Creative Leadership.

Hannum, K. M., & Hoole, E. (2009). *Tracking your development.* Greensboro, NC: Center for Creative Leadership.

Kirkland, K., & Manoogian, S. (1998). *Ongoing feedback: How to get it, how to use it.* Greensboro, NC: Center for Creative Leadership.

Martineau, J., & Hannum, K. (2004). *Evaluating the impact of leadership development: A professional guide.* Greensboro, NC: Center for Creative Leadership.

McCauley, C. D. (2006). *Developmental assignments: Creating learning experiences without changing jobs.* Greensboro, NC: Center for Creative Leadership.

Van Velsor, E., McCauley, C. D., & Ruderman, M. N. (Eds.). (2010). *The Center for Creative Leadership handbook of leadership development* (3rd ed.). San Francisco, CA: Jossey-Bass.

Ordering Information

TO GET MORE INFORMATION, TO ORDER OTHER IDEAS INTO ACTION GUIDEBOOKS, OR TO FIND OUT ABOUT BULK-ORDER DISCOUNTS, PLEASE CONTACT US BY PHONE AT 336-545-2810 OR VISIT OUR ONLINE BOOKSTORE AT WWW.CCL.ORG/GUIDEBOOKS.

Copyright © 2013 Center for Creative Leadership. All Rights Reserved.

Center for
Creative
Leadership·

Keep the learning
going by tapping
into CCL's **digital
development
solutions** which
provide **anytime**
access to world-class
tools and resources.

- Customized Blended Solutions
- In-House Solutions
- Lead 2.0
- Self-paced eCourses
- Digital Guidebook Library
- Webinars

CCL's array of digital learning products helps you build
leadership excellence when and where you need it most.
Learn more at www.ccl.org/digitallearning.

CPSIA information can be obtained
at www.ICGtesting.com
Printed in the USA
LVOW01s0859190117
521443LV00003B/4/P

9 781604 911725